TWO
MINUTES
TO
SHINE

Thirty Potent New Monologues for the
Auditioning Actor

by

PAMELA SACKETT

SAMUEL FRENCH, INC.
45 West 25th Street   NEW YORK 10010
7623 Sunset Boulevard HOLLYWOOD 90046
LONDON   TORONTO

IMPORTANT BILLING AND CREDIT REQUIREMENTS

All producers of TWO MINUTES TO SHINE *must* give credit to the Author of the Play in all programs distributed in connection with performances of the Play and in all instances in which the title of the Play appears for purposes of advertising, publicizing or otherwise exploiting the Play and/or a production. The name of the Author *must* also appear on a separate line, on which no other name appears, immediately following the title, and *must* appear in size of type not less than fifty percent the size of the title type.

CONTENTS

FOREWORD

How often does a performer get a chance to create a character of their own in a world of its own? *Two Minutes To Shine* allows exactly that. A highly original playwright, Pamela Sackett has put together an amazing set of monologues for men and women. This contemporary material ranges from funny to hilarious, sad to pathetic, satirical, dramatic--and always borders on quirky.

Any performer who has walked into an audition and seen that look on a director's face that says "there's *nothing* you can do that I haven't seen before *twice*" need have no fear. With this book, you can relax and relish material that is fresh and unique.

Certainly a book that offers everything from an hysterical woman mourning the loss of her monkey, a performer stopping a show to confront a patron's 'hissing snake,' to a tattoo artist with arthritis selling his business is a book to be cherished. As an actress, the most compelling aspect of this book is that the monologues are challenging. They are subtle, with a broad range of choices available to bring the characters to life. You will find something new every time you perform them; their depth and potential will grow and keep you growing as well. These monologues do indeed inspire you to dig your heels in, find the pearls, and craft your two minutes to shine.

My advice is to take them, enjoy and shine on.

--*Jacqueline Moscou*
Actor, Director, King County Arts Commissioner

MAKE UP YOUR MIND

a woman-in-love finally stands up for herself

How should I know where she's wandered off to?! What's the difference? *She* knows how to use a compass. She's not lost--Ginger never gets lost. She's exploring--and I'm in pain. But you don't seem to be too concerned about that. There are more *stumps* in this forest!

Would you put the map down please? I think it's time we talked about the fact that this whole arrangement isn't working out quite like I had hoped. How many more wild jaunts do I have to take with you and her before you make up your mind? I've been trying really hard because I believe that I am a lot righter for you than she is. I just wish you would give me the chance to prove it. It's not fair that every time we go away together, Ginger picks the place. Isn't it just a little odd that every place she picks happens not to be my cup of tea?

Is it so god-awful important to you that a woman operate a chain saw and milk a goat? If it is, then Ginger wins you hands down. How am I supposed to develop rural skills on the upper west side of Manhattan?! Do you really want me to start climbing trees instead of photographing them? My last nature photo won an award you know! But that's not enough for you--I have to join the forest service! This is ridiculous. If I'm not lovable to you the way I am, then, I . . . I don't know what to do.

I had a dream last night. It took me forever to finally fall asleep. I kept thinking Ginger's expert little campfire was going to ignite my sleeping bag. As soon as I dropped off, there you were asking me to haul water from a stream. You gave me this bucket full of holes. You kept demanding I bring you water, so I took the bucket down to the stream and there was Ginger, stark naked, spitting water like a fountain.

I realize now that dream was trying to tell me I'd be a lot happier in a Chinese restaurant which is where I'll be until you make up your mind. I don't need your map. It's about time I developed a better sense of direction.

DAMN!

an otherwise cooperative woman changes her mind

I don't care what you tell him. Just handle it--will you?! I thought I could go through with it, but I can't. I wish you had never told Francis I could do this. Why did you tell him I could do this?!

Don't look at me that way. I have every right to change my mind. I am entitled, any place, any time, to change my mind. And I am changing it right here and right now. Here and now, I have decided to refrain from popping out of that damn cake. I am no longer in the mood to have bing cherries dripping out of my ears.

I love the PTA. I am devoted to the PTA and the committee. And I realize the committee needs all the support they can get. That's why I agreed to do this in the first place. I'm so happy for them and I wanted to help celebrate their new budget; but there's got to be another way for them to kick up their heels without me covering myself with buttercream icing.

Please don't be angry with me, just help me get this window open. And before you wheel this thing out there, I want you to find Sam and somehow get that damn whistle away from him. There's no point in blowing it for an empty cake. It would be just like him to blow it anyway and make a big spectacle out of the fact that I changed my mind. Francis'll have a fit but what can he do--kick our kids out of school?

Do you realize if there had been one more woman on the committee, *you'd* be popping out of this cake instead of me?! I have a hunch neither one of us would have been invited to the party at all if I hadn't agreed to do this. I have a good mind to cut off their pencil supply.

Thank God this is a one-story house. Oh, and please do me a favor would you? Bring home what's left of the cake. I think I deserve a piece. I baked the damn thing!

PAY ATTENTION

neglected wife fights back

Are we speaking the same language or has your mind wandered off to Pluto again?! I wish you would pay attention to me when I talk. I am trying to tell you something. I think your tolerance for stimulation must be way up there because I know what I am saying to you is very interesting and you haven't blinked an eye. The company you keep during the day must be soooo electrifying that by the time you get home, your fuses have all blown. Is that it? Did you blow up real good today?! (*pause*) It's priorities then. Non-business-type relationships must be way down there. I'll bet I'm listed between "clean out the garage" and "feed the fish." Let's scroll on down and have a look--better yet--how about I pick up a copy of *Forbes* magazine and paste the pages all over my body. When you get done reading them, *we* could have a conversation--just you and I. I've got a better idea! What say I whip us up a little snack--how about a chocolate fondue? I'll light some violet candles, pour a couple shots of brandy, heat it, and then we could lay back and read the *Business Journal* to each other--out loud! Or, I could run out, right now, and take a crash course in economics. Then, we could have a delicious debate about the stock market. I'll bet that would put hair on the palm of your hands.

BANG!!! (*falls to floor*) Oh my god! I've shot myself! I've gone and shot my all alone self. Isn't that just a shame? Nobody around to help--I guess I'll just have to bleed to death. Nothing else to do. Can't sit around talking to myself for the **rest of my life!** Wait a second! Hang on! There's somebody coming towards me. Perhaps it's a medic. No. He can't be a medic. He's wearing a blue suit. Maybe he's a poet come to revive me with his, his *je ne sais quoi*. No, he can't be a poet. He looks too ordinary. Oh my god! It must be . . . yes, it's a businessman. A businessman is approaching and he looks like he means business. He's getting closer . . . closer still. Will he help me? Can he help me? Here he comes and . . . there he goes! (*a couple beats*) If you're looking for your calculator, I can't tell you where to find it but I'd sure like to tell you where you can put it!

HARD TO GET

a woman recounts a romantic traffic experience

It was like a dream. A great big beautiful carriage came rolling down the gray meadow. Actually, he drove a Chevy pickup and I caught my first glimpse of him on the freeway. He had a regal head with hair like an aura of black wispy clouds on either side of a shimmering river. Actually, he was a little bald on top with bushy hair around his ears. But those ears stuck out of his proud head held high like a crown upon a pedestal--a strong pedestal--his neck. So, it was a little on the thick side but there was no hair on it. His shoulders were round but he sat up straight for this man was not a slumper. His hands were strong as they gripped that steering wheel like the reins on a galloping steed. His voice was like a door opening--a little squeaky but he knew just what to say. "Get that hunk-a-metal off the road. I'm comin' up your tailpipe." He gunned his coughing motor, choked his clutch and spit fires of determination to intimidate my car off the road. Is this my prince in shining armor, I thought, as I gazed into my rear-view mirror dazzled by the sheen of his fully-receded hairline? I could see my reflection on his massive forehead and I was smiling. For once, I did not have to be the aggressor. I could sit back and watch a grown man make a total fool of himself. He was obviously in need of companionship and so was I. But this time, I was going to play hard to get.

"LEGS 'N' EGGS - KEEP 'EM MOVING!"

lovelorn woman at a worry clinic

Hello, Mrs. Mitzner. I don't mean to barge in on you but your secretary said your 10 o'clock didn't show and I *am* worried. I'm very worried. I've never been so worried--that's why I had to see you right away, Mrs. Mitzner. A friend of mine saw you last week and she's much better now--not worried about a thing anymore. She said she owes it all to your clinic. She told me all I have to do is pay in advance and my worries are over! 'Pay In Advance And Your Worries Are Over!' That's such a clever business motto. 'Pay in advance and' --oh. (*breaks out wallet and hands Mrs. Mitzner some cash, is instructed to be seated and sits down*) Thank you.

I got fired from my job today ... "Chicken Legs 'N' Eggs" -- that's the name of the place--all you can eat, no salad bars just the waitresses racing back and forth with these giant trays. I had great balance. Why, I could carry 317 legs at once--316 on one arm and I wiped my tears with the other. Never dropped one morsel of food either--got it out while it was still steaming.

... It wasn't my looks. He liked my looks just fine--for the restaurant--he thought a tall Russian* might bring people into the place. He couldn't tolerate the tears though. He said, "Ev". . . Ev-- it's short for Everything . . . Everything Bukinsky--that's my name . . . no, it was my father's idea. Anyway, my boss said, "Ev, you're doing a great job but you're getting my food wet and my customers are complaining about too much salt. If you don't stop crying on my food, I'll have to let you go." I tried, Mrs. Mitzner. I tried really hard not to cry. I'd stand in the kitchen with a tray full of steaming legs and eggs. The heat would rise up in my face and through the poultry mist, I could see Moe, my boss, the love of my life, looking every which way but never at me. I'd stand there with a tray of legs and a lump in my throat. Then I'd hear his voice--"Legs and Eggs!-- keep 'em moving!" The sound of his voice just got me and the moment I set foot onto the floor, I'd start gushing. I carried trays for five hours straight just to hear the sound of his voice-- "Legs and Eggs! Keep 'em moving!" I've got incredible stamina but I just couldn't stop crying.

I find chicken legs very depressing don't you? I used to dream about them. It was a recurring dream. Have you ever seen a chicken dance? Over and over again? Very depressing. And in this dream, Moe asked me to dance . . . with the legs! He wanted me to teach them how to dance over to his customers. He'd say, "Ev, show them how to serve themselves--this way you can cry all you want and my legs'll stay dry."

His precious food. He cared more about his legs than my feelings. I believe he really loved me deep down but he was married to that restaurant. He's full of chicken grease and he has a good heart--except when it comes to tall Russians. Why do people destroy what they love?

Adapt description as needed.

REMEDIAL 'HUSBANDRY'

'prim and proper' loses her patience

Please don't laugh. We are here to learn. I mean if somebody can't ask a question in this class then where, pray tell, can they ask it? Now Mr. Scott, I would like you to pose your question once again since Mr. Thalberg and Mr. Terry's laughter drowned out your voice half-way through. (*pause*) Come now, Mr. Scott--there's no need for embarrassment. (*pause*) Perhaps Mr. Thalberg or Mr. Terry would like to repeat your question for you? Their wives seem to be the most disturbed prior to their monthly 'visits.' Mr. Thalberg, Mr. Terry? (*pause*) Go ahead then, Mr. Scott, we're all waiting.

All right then, I'll speak up for you. Now correct me if I'm wrong but I believe you wanted to know why your wife insists on yelling non-sequiturs out the living room window while breaking eggs with her elbows just before that time of the month? It's not so important that you understand why she is doing this. It is more important, Mr. Scott, that you don't try to stop her from doing this. Self-expression is crucial for a woman during this particular time. A husband who attempts to stop his wife from expressing herself during this crucial phase of the moon, so to speak, barely lives to regret it. Modern man would be wise to accommodate a pre-menstrual female. Yes-- gone are the days when man got away with throwing his wife into a cave just because she bled for no apparent reason. Today we know exactly why she does this--don't we class?

Don't you know, Mr. Thalberg and Mr. Terry, that hysteria hampers the learning process? I would appreciate it if you would please control yourselves! I don't mean to reprimand you but you seem to need it so desperately! Perhaps you would like to share with the rest of the class what you think is so god-damned funny?! (*pause*) Then explain to me, if you will, why the two of you have enrolled in this class! Adult education is a marvelous thing--but you have to be an adult to appreciate it!! You have obviously not yet reached the point of maturity that enables you to do so!!! ... NO--I DO NOT HAVE MY PERIOD!!!! I'm beginning to think your wives don't either--not as often as you would like to believe. If you could experience such a thing, first hand, then the both of you could teach your own class!

(collecting herself) Next week, we will take a little trip to the grocery store and learn how to make an embarrassment-free purchase of assorted female paraphernalia. I would like Mr. Thalberg and Mr. Terry to be the first to try it.

OUT THERE

a secretary prolongs the inevitable

Don't say another word. I have to stop you or you'd go on another twenty minutes and you still wouldn't be able to say it. I could have made it easy for you. I know exactly what you're trying to tell me. I could have spoken up the moment we set foot in your office--your luxurious office. Sorry, I guess I wanted to see you squirm for a while. And I wanted to sit in your easy chair and catch this view one last time. I like this view. I've always liked this view. Every time I came in here for no matter what reason--even the times we rolled around on your fat desk--I always soaked in this view. I preferred it to your eyes. Besides, they were always closed. Did you think no one would notice if you kept them that way?

Did you really believe we could go on forever without someone getting wise out there? I mean, how many letters a day can one man dictate to his secretary and for how long? Do you realize that sometimes we'd be in here together for two hours straight and then I'd go back to my typewriter for ten minutes? And I'm a slow typist. Everyone knows that. So what if I was in here all day? I was only doing my job. Is that any reason to fire me?

Do you think firing me will stop them from talking or keep your wife from finding out? It's a little late for that. You're the only one with their head in the sand. But you know, I'm glad the word is out far enough for you to notice. It's all out in the open now. No more sneaking around. Now you know that they know. That was the biggest secret. They know. They've known for a long time. Oh, don't worry. They don't know everything. But maybe they should. Maybe I should set them straight before I go. I'll bet all the secretaries out there who, in their roundabout way, are pressuring you to get rid of me are jealous and think they want to take my place. That's because they all think they know what went on behind these doors. But they don't.

Should I tell them about all your dispassionate passion? That oughta deflate their aspirations. Maybe I should tell them about all the hours you laid on that couch, alone, while I sat next to you on the floor and listened to your marital woes long after five P.M. I could also tell them about all our Saturday afternoons in the park that lasted all of three seconds because your kid needed a last minute ride to her dance lesson or your wife was expecting you for lunch at the Brasserie. I must tell them how very generous you are and how lucky I was to have been the recipient of one whole greeting card every holiday season and one red geranium for birthdays fresh from my own window box. Would any one of those gum-crackers out there be willing to put up with that? I'll bet not! If you were smart, you'd fire everybody *but* me! *They're* replaceable. Maybe you won't have to fire anybody at all. Because after I fill everyone in on the details, we'll all quit!

I'D LIKE TO STRANGLE YOU

innovative musician takes revenge

What's wrong? Don't you recognize me? Let me refresh your memory. I'm the one with the clumsy fingers. Isn't that what you called them? (*pulls newspaper clipping from pocket*) No, I was wrong. You called them stumbling fingers. (*focusing more closely on clipping*) "Stumbling, stubby fingers!" I'd like to strangle you with these stubby fingers.

I have practiced with these stumbling, stubby fingers since I was four years old. We're talking twenty-five years. What have you been doing with *your* fingers for the last twenty-five years?

Listen up Mr. I-always-wanted-to-be-a-musician-but-I-never-had-the-talent-or-the-discipline-so- I -think- I'll -make-a-living-bashing-people-who-do Hollingsworth! I am playing the *new* music, Mr. I-have-lost-my-childlike-spontaneity-because- I've-been-reviewing-old-music-for-so-long-my-ears-are-musty Critic! I realize the *new* music is just a bit disorienting to a stagnant ear. It probably confused you so much that you thought I was making a mistake a minute at last night's concert but I'll have you know every note I played last night was planned. It's not my fault you were in the mood for Beethoven. My parents were in the mood for Beethoven too which is why they didn't come to my concert last night. They never come to my concerts but they do read your column. My father called me just this morning to say that he and my dear ma-ma read your review and want me to reimburse them for all that money they spent on all those lessons. My parents are soooo funny when they feel humiliated.

I'm funny too, and so are my buddies--the ones standing outside your door like guard dogs waiting to break your fingers for bad-mouthing mine. Yeah, they're just dying to get in here and rearrange your taste in music but I told them I could get you to write a retraction instead. You've got eight minutes, Hollingsworth. Write a retraction or go into traction. What's it gonna be?

SPIT THEM OUT

a patient struggles for clarity

I told you, doctor. This one looks like a giraffe with a washing machine on top of his head and that one looks like a giraffe with a washing machine coming out of his mouth. Does that mean I'm sick? I mean I know these ink blots aren't really supposed to look like anything, but, I don't think they're supposed to look like that!

I mean, what is it I'm projecting here? This giraffe with a washing machine on top of his head could mean, in my mind, that life is a burden. Look at that washing machine! It's a lot bigger than the giraffe's head. But wait a second! The neck isn't breaking. It's still sticking straight up. The giraffe doesn't look too happy but at least his neck isn't breaking. That's a good sign, isn't it doctor? He's got this heavy machine on top of his head but he hasn't keeled over or anything.

Maybe the machine signifies the giraffe's brain--my brain really. I've never thought of myself as a giraffe but that's the beauty of these tests. They really help you get at your true self-image. I'm not as tall as a giraffe but maybe I feel tall deep down or want to be tall or maybe I think I'm taller than I actually am. That's good doctor. Don't you think? That's really good.

I think the washing machine itself represents the giraffe's actual thoughts--my thoughts. They do spin around. Maybe I want to wash them away or spit them out like in that picture where the other giraffe is throwing up. Maybe the fact that I saw that in the second sequence means I'm getting ready to fight back. I'm not going to let these thoughts burden me. I'm going to spit them out. And that's what I've been doing. Right doctor?! I've been spitting them out for six months.

And look! This washing machine that the giraffe is spitting out looks like it's about to land in somebody's lap. I'll bet that's your lap, doctor. Oh look! The lap is just on the edge of the page. Looks like the lap is on its way out of the picture. That must mean I don't want to see you anymore. You think that's it, doctor? I don't want to see you? Now that's really strange because I had a feeling I might feel that way--like I don't want to see you. I think I might not want to see you anymore. And that's why I saw the blot that way. I don't want to see you. What do you think, doctor?

MY TABLE

a bookworm celebrates romance and a personal victory

Please go ahead. Order anything on the menu. It's my treat. Tonight I want you to satiate your appetite like you never have before. Knock yourself out. Don't get the same old snack. I want you to order the works. I just love how they have a separate menu for every course. Do you like the flowers? I ordered them over the phone so if the french is misspelled, it's not my fault. Incidentally, this is the exact same table on which we first ate together three-and-a-half weeks ago. I asked them to move it from the corner. Can you believe it? I'm ready to dine in front of everybody tonight. Amazing isn't it? I thought the corner might be more romantic since that's exactly where I was sitting when you first came over. No more corners for me though.

I'm so glad you came over to my table that night--that fateful night. Look! It's still got scratches on the edge from when you first came over. I was so nervous. I kept digging my fork into the wood. You thought I ate like a bird. The truth was my fork was full of splinters and I was embarrassed to ask for another one. Have I told you how very glad I am that you came over to my table that night? You persistent little bugger, you.

I never did finish that book. I put away a trilogy at this very table just a week before you came over. My reading habits changed the moment I met you. So did everything else.

If it weren't for that training, I wouldn't be sitting here with you tonight. I never thought I'd get up the nerve to go to that School For The Shy And Apprehensive. Tuesday night was my last class. It was a thrill. I turned in my turtle pin. The head of the school gave a beautiful speech about how a star pupil of hers was approached by somebody in the corner of a restaurant and actually asked him/her to sit down--*two times*! I blushed. That just gave me away. They all wanted to know who you were and what the name of the restaurant was. I just couldn't tell them--not because I'm apprehensive--I just don't want them trying out their new skills on you.

Oh my god, the head of that school just walked in the front door. Please promise me you won't tell her that when I first asked you to sit down, I meant at another table.

I CAN'T HEAR YOU

an actor stops mid-play to reprimand a noisy audience

Can you please take your snake out of this theatre?! (*to cast*) I'm sorry everybody. I love this play and everyone in the cast has been so good and so good to me. This whole town has been good to me but I had to stop. (*toward audience*) Has your snake read the reviews?! They were glowing. And understandably so, but when, in a play, as an actor, I am in the throes of a climactic moment and my fellow actors are working with me in close proximity, fighting for their very breath to reach that truth, that life-threatening flame of sincerity, and I hear a snake in the audience, hissing loudly, I have to say somebody on the staff made a grave error.

It's not that I have anything against rare and exotic pets. One of my closest friends has a rat but she never brings it to the theatre! I think every living being should be exposed to culture. I'd be the first to vote for equal rights and an open door policy but this is ridiculous!

(turns back to proceed with play)

What do you mean he's dead?! Did you say dead? Did I hear those dreaded words pass over your tongue and lips? Tell me the words. Say them again so that I may hear them loud and distinct and unmistakable--those wrenching syllables like a great and crushing instrument bearing down on my sunken chest. Say them again. I dare your mouth to form the words, the utterances, to spit the sounds like hard nails driving into my heart. What is this? You cannot speak? Are you whispering? Speak up! I can't hear you over the sound of that hissing snake in the audience!!

(turns back towards audience)

If you don't tell your snake to shut up, I'm going to shut down this theatre and you, the snake owner, will have to return every cent invested in this play to your fellow audience members. And that goes for those of you out there who have been rattling candy wrappers, programs and newspapers. And those of you coughing, moving around in your seats and talking amongst yourselves might want to chip in a few bucks to also reimburse the cast for their time and trouble. Good evening!

ABOUT MY LAWN
terminally repressed award recipient minces words

Thank you all so very much. I am thrilled and, may I say, I am so honored and tickled and touched by this grand gesture. It is a true treat to be singled out by the city council, especially when you work so hard like I have and for so long. When somebody finally sits up and takes notice, it just makes everything I have done to deserve this award well worth the time and trouble.

And it is so special to be the very first person on my street to receive an award--albeit the only person. When the decision was made to give this award, I jumped for joy not just because I knew I would be the recipient but because the focal point of this special honor has been sadly passed over for years by everybody--especially the people on my street. Not a one on my street has ever said a word to me--about my lawn. When the council announced their decision, I was so proud just to be a resident in the very first suburb that finally got its priorities straight. It's about time everybody realized that manicured lawns do make a difference.

The council fights so hard to maintain order, the least we citizens can do is cut the grass. Well-cut grass is only the beginning though. We need awards for well-trimmed hedges and trees and flowers. Have you seen mine lately?

Happiness is in your own backyards, you see, and an orderly yard, a well-kept yard, is the key to peace in our city. I hope to be an inspiration to all of you who have overlooked your yards completely. If only one other person on our street sat up and took notice of my lawn, perhaps that person would have felt encouraged to ask me how I do it so that they could do it and then I would have someone to share this award with. It would be my pleasure to share this award with somebody--anybody. Perhaps my offer to share this award will be incentive to one of you.

In closing, I would like to say that I would be more than happy to help any resident on my street get started on their yard. As you know, I am home, alone, everyday. Just give me a call.

DOWN THERE

an employee verges on suicide

You think this is easy? Go on--go back to your throne and don't try to talk me out of it! I don't want you to. Can you hear them down there? That's the most encouragement I've had since I was sixteen. I was up here once before, you know? It was a different building, of course, but the feeling was the same. The crowd's changed too but the enthusiasm is no different. They *want* me to do it! Oh yes! They want to see blood and this time, I'm going to give it to them. Look at all those hungry faces down there. That's what I like to do just before I go for it. I like to see those hungry faces just before I let 'er rip and fly through the air.

(*starts to lose balance, nearly falls, then regains equilibrium*)

Don't you come out here. Don't you dare come out here or I'll do it right now. That's right. *You* listen to me for a change. Aren't I the powerful one now? You didn't know how powerful I was when you hired me did you? You thought I'd obey you every step of the way just like the rest of your saluting staff of sheep! That's what they are, too. You say, "BOO!" and they say "BAAAAA!" I'll bet they make you feel downright almighty. But I'm the one now. I've got the whole world in the palm of my hand. Look at them down there-- hundreds of them just waiting for ME! And you, the head of the herd, taking precious time out of your busy day just to watch me do it.

It took me years to get this brave again--brave enough to really do it--this time. Working for *you* is the *easy* way out. But I found my guts today and you can have 'em. They'll be all over Third Street in a few minutes. Oh, incidentally--I quit!

EVERY YEAR

brother Carl does it again

Yes, I'm surprised! Of course I'm surprised! If you walked into your own dark, empty house, turned on the light and found a room full of screaming people, wouldn't you be surprised? You can stop screaming now. Please stop screaming.

Thank you all for coming. My brother Carl sure knows how to throw a surprise birthday party, doesn't he? I can see he's covered everything--the cake, the candles, the punch, the balloons, and this year it looks like he's sprung for multi-colored name tags. Thank you so much for wearing them.

You look like interesting people and very generous, too. That's the biggest stack of presents I've ever seen. I keep telling Carl, "Please, if you're going to ask a group of total strangers to come over and celebrate my birthday with me, do not ask them to bring gifts. Their very presence will be gift enough."

But Carl insists, every year, on coming up with a whole new set of very giving strangers. Where did you find them this year, Carl? Hasn't been a familiar face in the bunch since I was thirteen. And you know why? Because my brother Carl hates my friends. He's never approved of them not since I was thirteen. When I was thirteen, I wanted to invite my own friends to my birthday party but he wanted to invite somebody else's. He didn't like my friends then and he doesn't like them now. He hates their guts, actually, and he thinks he knows better than me who I should hang out with. Every year, he hand picks a group of people that he thinks would be a good influence on me. And every year, I tell him to drop dead and leave me alone. I hate his taste in people and I can tell in one glance his taste hasn't changed. *That* doesn't surprise me at all.

So drink up everybody. Help yourself to some cake, have a few laughs, open up my presents and give them to yourselves--enjoy my house. Carl, I'll be at Esther's again! You've got two hours to clean up. I'm expecting a few friends over tonight.

NEVER! NEVER! NEVER!

a mourner shares loss with sympathetic ear

I know it was important. Graduation parties are always important. I realize that and I want you to know I had every intention of coming but ... I don't think it would have been right for me to go out and celebrate because Anderson died last night. (*pause*) Go ahead--laugh. Laugh your nervous laugh. Get it out of your system. I know how upset you must feel--deep down--I mean you weren't exactly close to him, but I know how much you wanted to be. Go ahead--laugh right out loud--it'll make you feel better--I'll wait. (*long pause and then loudly bursting into tears*) Oh Anderson! (*pulling self together*) We were so happy together! (*falling apart*) Why did he have to leave me!! (*pinching self together*) I have plenty of my own, thanks. (*pulls tissues out of pocket in rapid succession and blows nose with fervor*)

I'll never find anyone like him again. Never never never! Oh I know what you're going to say. There are other monkeys in this world but I don't want another monkey! (*bursting out again*) I want my Andersooooooooooon!!! (*pulling self together*) No! I hate ferrets. I don't want to go back to reptiles! (*bursting out*) I want my monkey!!

(*pulling self together with abruptness*) So--how was your party? (*pause, then angrily*) No. I don't want to go to the zoo! (*starting to lose control again but gets a grip on self and continues*) So--how was your party? Was Jeff there? Oh, wait a minute. (*holding on for dear life*) Don't talk about Jeff--he reminds me of Anderson. (*starting to gush a bit*) He reminds me so much of Anderson! (*yanking self together*) I can't think about it. I'd better go or I'll be late to the service. (*falling apart*) Would you like to take one last look? Oh never mind. I don't think you can handle it.

NO MORE!

long-time resident protects her territory

I'm not going to move. You can't make me! I am going to sit right here for as long as I have to. I'm not going to budge until you go away for good and it would be in your best interest to go before you try to destroy what's left of my neighborhood.

I watched those giant jaws of yours eat up two buildings now. I saw my neighbor's hallway hanging by a thread just before her entire building collapsed. I used to walk through that hallway to visit my neighbor--my friend, Lily.

You see that yellow chair in the rubble? That was one of her chairs. I sat in it for hours. That was my favorite chair. I liked it better than the one I got in my place. I spent hours in that chair drinking tea and talking to my pal. She was always there when I needed her--until you came along and destroyed the building next to hers.

She coughed from the dust and destruction and then she developed some respiratory problems. She cried herself to sleep every night. We could hear her wailing late into the night. Then we all got those letters. Lily asked me to read hers and tell her what it said but I was afraid to. I didn't have the heart to tell her what those damn letters of yours had to say. None of us could tell Lily. Everybody knew she was too frail to take such bad news.

I layed awake all night praying you'd never come. I prayed for Lily's sake. I stopped praying the day you carried her out. I vowed to myself I'd never pray again. She looked so peaceful. They said she died from old age but I know it was because Lily just didn't want to live in a world where they do this to good people.

So I'm going to sit right here until you go away. Take your lunch pails and your outhouses and your machines and you go if you know what's good for you. You see the top windows on my building? There's a pair of eyes peeping out of every one of those windows up there and they ain't lookin' for the lord! They're looking at you and your machines. If you take one more step--if you so much as even try to touch me or move me from this pile of dirt, my neighbors, what's left of them, and what's left is the angriest, most ornery bunch, are going to let you have it like you never had it before. There'll be no more demolishing around here or my fearless comrades up there are going to demolish you! I'll bet those machines of yours cost a pretty penny--all we have to lose is a few rounds of ammunition. I said don't take another step ... all right neighbors let 'em have it!!

TWO MINUTES TO SHINE

determined actor takes liberties while fighting
over-bearing parental influence

Hello? Excuse me. Hello. Are you ready for me? Please stop writing--please. I mean I know the person who auditioned before me was probably great and everything and gave you all sorts of ideas on how you want to cast this play but I'm here now and we only have so much time. Besides, I'm not here to give you ideas. I'm here to knock you out of your chair!

I want to tell you that I am filled with the muses--numerous muses--some very dark and compelling, others buoyant and gleeful! I am and have always been bursting with the muses and I feel most confident that my abilities can inspire *your* abilities to cast this play with someone like me--someone exactly like me--*me*!

But I got a phone call from my mother last night. I was right in the middle of working on this brilliant piece for you. I told her, "Mother, please, I've only got five hours to prepare for this two minute audition and I am just on the brink of nailing down my through line. Can you call me back later?" She said, "Two minutes?! Is that all the time they're giving you to demonstrate your genius? Two minutes?! I'm sorry," she said, "but my baby needs more than two minutes to shine!" Can you believe that?! She said it was a crime to condense all my talents down to just two minutes. "Marlon/Marlena," she said, "you can shine a pair of shoes in two minutes but you are not a pair of shoes. You are a masterpiece! You are my child! You are the sun, the stars, the moon and the only person on earth who never calls me." She went on and on until the lines in my script looked like little snakes in heat and I told her so and then I threatened to cancel my audition. So she made me promise to show up and arrange to come back after the snakes turned back into words which is why I'm here.

Despite what my mother thinks, I just know I can show you what I got in two minutes if you would just give me two minutes a week from Thursday. I promise I won't take a second over two minutes of your time. It will be the most thrilling two minutes you have ever spent. Please--bring your sunglasses!

OLD FACE

dissatisfied customer barges in on plastic surgeon

I want my face back, Dr. Deutsch! Do you hear me? I want it back! You took it away from me and I want it back now. I don't want this face. I know I paid you for it. I don't care about the money. It's not the money. It's just I want my old face back.

Put the phone down--your secretary is tied up--literally. I know guns. I spent the last six weeks learning guns--ever since I called and your secretary told me you were booked up for months. I can't wait for months. I want my old face back right now.

You told me I'd have a whole new lease on life. What does that mean, Dr. Deutsch? I wanted new looks not new peers. I liked my peers. I miss my wonderful old friends. They can't stand to look at me now because it makes them feel old. I feel just like them but I don't fit in anymore, Dr. Deutsch.

That's why I want it back. You can have your new lease and you can have all my new friends, too. I don't want them. They're pretty to look at but they're stupid. They think the world revolves around them and they don't understand why I want to hang out with old people. I wish I could tell them why but I can't.

I just want to undo it now. I've got the money and you've got the skills. I want you to put the years back into my face--every wrinkle. And I want you to do it right now or I'll go out to that waiting room full of people and tell them they're paying for a new face but they're buying a desert island.

SHE SAID

desperate mate tries to justify break-up

I went to my psychic again today and she told me we aren't going to make it. She said every time I set foot in her office she sees doors and between my first appointment and my seventh, the doors grew. She said, today I was on one side and you were on the other. She said a month ago, the door was wide open. Today, it was open a crack and she saw my hand in a fist around the knob. She told me that she could hear the door about to slam and it was deafening. Then she explained to me that this was an audio-prophesy and if we get out of this relationship now, it won't hurt either one of us so much later.

I think we should listen to her and start packing. I don't think either one of us should feel rejected either. It's not like we *want* to break up. We've been getting along great--I thought. But a warning is a warning and I just don't think we should turn our backs on this kind of thing. This psychic has proven herself several times over. Remember the first time I went to her and she kept saying, "Orange! Orange! I see orange!"? And then I got this incredible head cold two weeks later and there was a sale on oranges and I told you to buy three pounds? There is no doubt in my mind those oranges cured me!

I asked her what would happen if we ignored the warning and went on as we are. She immediately crossed her eyes, gazed up into her forehead and said that she couldn't see the doors anymore but she could see this big hole and it was black and out of focus and then our time was up. She advised me to make another appointment because it was crystal clear to her third eye that after you and I split up, I would definitely need some guidance. And she said you would too. So, I made an appointment for you. I hope you don't mind.

SOMETHING'S UP

sibling rivalry at its worst

You haven't seen me or talked to me for two weeks. Got it? They won't discover his body until some time tomorrow. He was supposed to play raquetball, as usual, with Fagen at noon. When Fagen finds him, and I'm sure he will, you're going to be the first person he calls so get ready to lie. You were always good at that. That's how I know I can trust you to protect me. Remember--you haven't seen me or talked to me for two weeks. I've got my alibi all prepared but I doubt I'll need one. Everybody knows I was devoted to my brother so I'll be the last one they suspect.

I'll get ahold of you later. I can't tell you where I'm going to be. I know you'd be tempted to go there and that would just blow everything. They'll be following you for a while and tapping your calls. So you're going to have to put on a confident face--more confident than the one you've got on right now--a lot more confident.

And you should be happy too--not outwardly, of course. Outwardly, you'd better look pretty darn grief-stricken or else they'll know something's up--but inside, you should be real happy. Alan was a pain to both of us and I couldn't stand to see him hurt you anymore. I love my mother too much to stand by and watch her suffer. Well, your suffering days are over. I'll be back by the time they read the will. Then we can go out and celebrate--just you and I!

You should have seen him. It was the first time in years he wasn't answering the phone, running off to a meeting, or punching up his calculator. All it took was two bullets and he calmed right down. I've never seen him so relaxed. You would have been proud of him, Mother. Go on over and have a look. Today Alan is ready to listen to you when you talk. And he'll never talk back to you again. I guarantee it!

WE'RE TOGETHER NOW

a woman/man relays annoying phone call to mate

You got a phone call. It was about two hours ago and I told her/him I didn't know when you'd be back. I knew who it was even though s/he wouldn't leave her/his name. I asked her/him for it. I was very nice about it, too. I told her/him I'd be more than happy to take a message and I'd be sure to see that you got it.

S/he tried disguising her/his voice and it sounded like s/he was covering the mouthpiece with a kleenex. S/he must think I'm really stupid. S/he was pretending s/he had a cold, too. S/he kept clearing her/his throat and sniffling. S/he tried to sound real official like s/he was calling from an insurance company or something. S/he thinks I'm stupid.

Why couldn't s/he just be straightforward about it? It's not like we don't know of each other. I'd recognize that voice anywhere. I've heard it thirty-six times now.

Why does s/he keep calling you? What does s/he want? Doesn't s/he realize that we're together now? S/he must know we're together. Every time s/he calls *I* answer the phone.

Next time s/he calls, I'm going to tell her/him that you told me to tell her/him that s/he'd better not call you anymore. Next time s/he calls and says, "That's quite all right, I'll phone him/her again later," I'm going to say to her/him, "Patricia/Patrick, don't phone again later because Tony/Tanya told me to tell you that he/she never wants to talk to you or see you again!" Isn't that right? I'm going to tell her/him flat out, next time, to leave you alone. OK?! I think s/he'll get the message and give up--don't you?

Where have *you* been all day? I'm not stupid y'know?!

HELPLESSLY, HOPELESSLY

man/woman interrupts a wedding ceremony

Excuse me, but I can't hold my peace or my tongue--not now and certainly not forever. I've lived next to the bride/groom for the past two-and-one-half months and if this couple takes the leap now, they're going to need one hell of a net in the near future, because I'm in love with her/him. And I know Rhonda/Randall feels the same way about me. S/he is the sweetest, most sensitive wo/man I've ever met. S/he has the compassion of a saint and that's why, to this day, Fred/Frieda has had no knowledge of our relationship. S/he bent over backwards to protect him/her.

But I can't live a lie and I would never lie in a church. I think it's all that stained glass and those images of angels and martyrs. Well, if Rhonda/Randall wants to play martyr, I'll play angel of mercy and lift Fred/Frieda off that hook of despair to which he/she would have had to look forward if I hadn't come here today.

You'll thank me, Fred/Frieda--not now and perhaps not for years to come, but, one day, down the road, you'll look back on all this and know that graciously stepping aside was the only right thing to do. There's no point in hating us. Could we help it if we fell helplessly and hopelessly in love with each other? God knows and you must know too that Rhonda/Randall is one of those rare and irresistible gems and the forces that pulled us together were more powerful than the raging sea.

Fate has a funny way of knocking on your door when you least expect it and it's knocking on your door, Fred/Frieda. Please answer it and laugh.

LATE BILLS

a customer tries to fast-talk bureaucracy into submission

Well, who is the person in charge?! Wait a minute! Why didn't you tell me you weren't the person in charge? I can't believe you didn't tell me. Damn it! You mean I have to tell this whole story all over again to somebody else? I can't go through this again. Why didn't you tell me the minute I started talking to you that you are not the one who handles late bills? Why did you let me go on like that? You must find me altogether fascinating or why else would you let me go on about it? You probably didn't hear a word I said. Well don't stand there like a statue--go get the person in charge. I said go get--

(*to self*) I can't go through this story all over again. (*paces impatiently*)

Who are you? Are you the person in charge? Are you sure? Prove it. Wait a minute. Don't go. I'm sorry. I'm tired. I just went through my entire situation from beginning to end and then your assistant woke up and told me that I bore my soul to the wrong person. That's after waiting in line for three hours after driving around for two until I finally found a parking space--it was more like a parking puddle. My dress/suit was pink/blue when this day began. And after all that, I have to do it all over again?--not the driving or the parking but the telling of every last legitimate reason why I haven't paid this bill yet; and there you are, finally, the person in charge, waiting to hear all about it but I'm just too tired and upset to repeat it.

So because of all the trouble you put me through--all the ineptitude and negligence and bad parking--I think it would be only fair not to charge me for this one long distance call I made by mistake and to give me another extension on this bill which I have every intention of paying. If your assistant had been listening, he could tell you the reasons why I can't pay this bill yet. They are excellent reasons and totally understandable. If you had heard them, you would have to agree with me. And if he had heard them, I'm sure he would agree with you. So, since we all agree with each other, I think I'll go home now. I'm expecting a call. OK? Very good meeting you and have a pleasant afternoon.

OFF THE BAT

jealous lover with good reason

I lost my head. It happens--you know? Lots of people lose their heads. I lost mine. That's not why I came over here. I didn't come over to lose my head. That wasn't my plan at all. I just planned to come over. I never planned to use the key but I had to get in. And then I got to thinking about how I was here and you weren't. That's what did it. I was here and you weren't. That's what I got to thinking right off the bat. But then I thought I should give it the benefit of the doubt--off the bat.

You see, I walked in and called out your name. Not right off. I knocked first, of course, and you didn't answer. So I took your key out from under and that's when I walked in and called out your name and you didn't answer. That's when I began to lose my head. I *thought* I was losing my head but, like I said, I wanted to give it the benefit of the doubt so I ripped your place apart. I thought, maybe, just maybe, you were lost like my head--under your furniture or behind your paintings or down the basement or in your drawers. I had no idea you were hiding in your bed with--sorry, I didn't catch your name?

You should've answered. I don't like it when you don't answer-- especially when I call out your name. When I call out somebody's name, anybody's name, and no one answers, I lose my head! It just gets away from me and that's why I tore everything up. I had to look for my head and I had to look for you. I lost my head and I lost you all at the same time. Funny how that works.

You know how they say things happen in threes? That means we got one more thing to lose. What did you say your name was? . . . BINGO! Somebody lost their voice.

THAT BOY

apologetic parent grabs at straws

He didn't mean to say that. I swear I don't know where he got that language. We don't even own a TV. And I keep that boy away from magazines of all kinds--except the *Watchtower*.

I'm real sorry about the side of your car. I just can't imagine where he got that can of spray paint. We don't keep nothin' around the house like that. Maybe you could park your car the other way around until you remove the paint, though. I just can't bear to look at what he wrote on it--can you? That boy can't spell worth a damn!

And I'm just sick about your dog. If I told that boy once, I told him a thousand times, keep your mitts off my garden tools. Those clippers'll just never be the same. But don't you fret none. Your dog's tail's bound to grow back *one* of these days. Sassy's did. Took a while, but Sassy's tail came back better than the one she had before. Not as long, of course, but when she waggles it somethin' back there moves.

And listen here, I'd be happy to help you reorganize that garage of yours as soon as you lug all your stuff in off the street. That boy's idea of exercise is beyond me. Anyhow, I can help lug your stuff in after I lug in mine. Maybe you could help me lug mine in first. We can help each other. That's what neighbors are for! Uh, but don't worry, I won't ask you to watch the boy again for a while. Not until he learns more manners.

Besides, the Parkers are back from their vacation now and they said they're rested up and ready to watch the boy again. They put their basement back in order and moved the deadbolt out of that boy's reach so the rest of the house can be safe and secure this time.

If only I didn't have to travel so much. I could stay home with the boy myself. If only I had the time. I could teach him what to do with all his energy. That boy's got more energy than he knows what to do with. Well, he knows what to do with it, I just wish he wouldn't do it so often.

I GOT FEELIN'S

a man tries to convince his wife not to leave him

What do you mean I can't feel?! Who are you? The Queen of Hearts? I got feelin's. I don't have to prove anything to you, but if I had to prove it, I could. Believe you me, I could prove my feelin's.

Who cried when the Dodgers blew it? (*sarcastically*) I don't have feelin's?! And when that punk stole my tool box? You remember--I left the garage door open once. Just once, but that's all it took--brand new wrench and those needle-nose pliers! I loved those pliers with all my heart. But I don't have feelin's--right! And when they canceled the game on account-a lousy weather? I was full of feelin's that day.

You think you're so sensitive with your moods galore. I'd be moody too if I had all those hormones flyin' around. You think you're so sensitive. You just got nature on your side. What did nature ever do for me?

I got feelin's no matter what you say and I know my rights, but you don't care. You with your feelin's walkin' out that door when I-- when I need to have you *not* walk out that door. What did you hear me say just now? Did I say need? Yes, I did--I need you *not* to walk out that door. You see? I got feelin's and I got the feelin' that if you walk out that door, I won't be feelin' too good. And I don't like *that* feelin'.

I got things to do. My business don't run itself and it don't run on feelin's. I get up every morning whether I *feel* like it or not. What do you do? You and your feelin's. Do your feelin's pay the rent? No--I pay the rent! And what if I walked up to the landlord and said, "I don't feel like it this month?" You say that to me all the time! There you have it. I'm more sensitive than the landlord and she's a woman. Don't that beat all?

Never mind--go ahead. I'll get over it--or maybe I won't. Maybe I got so many feelin's that I'll never recover. But I don't have to prove anything to you about that. So why don't you stay put and we can both of us wonder who's got more feelin's. And let's leave the game playin' to the Dodgers. OK?!

CHIRP! CHIRP! CHIRP!

a groom-to-be in flight from his wedding

You saved my life! Do you realize that? I am forever indebted and you don't even know me. What possessed you to help me out like that? You must have read my mind. Was that it? You read my mind. I've never had so much trouble opening a door. I think the lock was jammed from the inside. You got the magic fingers though. It was locked from the inside wasn't it? Ahhh, what's the difference? You got it opened and I can't thank you enough.

I couldn't go through with it, you see? I just couldn't bring myself to--you know? Of course you know. *You* got me out of there. This calls for a friendship--a permanent friendship--and a drink. Would you like to have a drink with me? I'm thirsty all of a sudden. That was a hell of a squeeze. Took all the moisture out of me--out of my mouth anyway. What do you say? I'd like to talk to you a while. Or we can just keep driving. Let's drive for a while. OK?

What a trip. I can't believe it. I'll try anything once. That's what I always say. You ever been married? Yeah, me neither--except today--*(laughs)*--well, almost today. I just don't get it. Can't a person love somebody without spending their whole life proving it? . . .Yeah, I think so too. Not Gwen though. With Gwen you have to sign your whole life away. I never have understood this commitment thing. You know what kind of people are committed? Prisoners and crazy people, that's who. Boy, are those guys ever tied down. Not me. I'm a free man. Free as a bird. Chirp, chirp, chirp. That's me-- free as a bird. I can chirp away as long and as loud as I like now. And if they don't like it--lump it. That's what I say.

She'll never speak to me again I bet. It's not my fault her folks spent all that damn money. I told her not to let 'em. I wanted a small wedding, but they wouldn't take no for an answer. Pushy people sure run up a bill for themselves don't they? I'll be damned if I'm gonna be told what to do by somebody else's parents. I don't even listen to my *own* parents. I should've listened to them this time though. Dang! Now I'll *have* to listen to them forever and a day. *(mimicking self-righteous voice)* "I told you so!" Shoot! They told me I wouldn't go through with it.

How long've we been driving? I bet she's still getting into that $500 dress her daddy bought her. Probably just now putting on the veil. She looked beautiful in that thing. I snuck a peek the night they were fixing the headband on it. She looked beautiful. Her cheeks were bright pink. They get that way when she's real nervous --like the first time I asked her out or every time she discovers I've been staring at her from across the room. Yeah--those cheeks were real pink that night. They just glowed through her veil and those eyes of hers--they can read your mind. And she's got this infectious giggle. All I have to do is give her one of my looks and she . . . .

Shoot! Can you give me a lift back to that place? Feel like going to a wedding today? I'd like you to be my guest. I'd like you to help me with the door again. Chirp!

CAPTAIN KICH

nostalgic tattooist selling his shop

Welcome to Captain Kich's Custom Tattoo and Snack Bar. Well, if you're interested, you can call it what you want. You don't have to keep the name. But if you buy the place, it'd be to your advantage to use my name. It's gonna cost a little extra, of course, but it'll pay off in the end. I got the best reputation in the neighborhood. Won't be a dry eye on the block after I go. Ask Madame Cooch--two doors down. She sells boas. You know, those frilly things you wrap around the neck? Madame Cooch says the rest of 'em are all hacks. I'm the real thing. That Tattoo and Body Piercing Emporium one block over? What a joke! Most of their customers come straight to me after an appointment with those people. Why just last month a couple came in with matching tattoos from that place. They wanted twin apes holding the American flag. What did they get from the Emporium? Looked like purple confetti flappin' around in a mud puddle. Birth marks! That's what their tattoos look like. Nope--I'm the artist around these parts. I got a certificate of excellence from the Shelton School of Picture Framing, I took a class on Lithuanian literature and I have attended five seminars on skin care. You gotta keep up on things to run this parlor right.

And that I have. Why, long about nine P.M., this place is hoppin'. "Brewin' and bruisin'. " That's what they'd say, "We're brewin' and a-bruisin'." My customers teased me, but everybody knew I had the steadiest hand around and it was always a painless operation. They'd say, "Give it your best shot, Captain." "Lay it on me." "I'll have some of that easy-does-it epidermal imagery!" That's what they'd say. They'd come in, grab a stool and a brew and put their arms on the bar. Or they'd stretch out on that old dentist chair over there in the corner. For chest, face, or rear jobs, I got me a good flat table in the back room--comes with the place. So does that old popcorn machine. I'd keep that thing goin' 'round the clock. My customers always wanted somethin' to chew on when the needle went in--kept 'em thirsty too.

Yep, I've made my mark around these parts. I heard you got what it takes too--else I wouldn't be willin' to sell ya my name. I got my standards to uphold--even after I'm gone, I got my standards. I hear you got a fine sense of aesthetics. I can appreciate your specialty too. I hear tell your customers will follow you anywhere for a hubcap-on-the-hip. Hubcaps on the hip--sure is a sign of an original thinker--and that you are. I think we're 'bout the only ones left around here. Yep--I think you're just right to take over my place.

Captain Kich's Custom Tattoo and Snack Bar has seen the likes of 'em all--all kinds. And I've done all types o' tattoos too. My very first customer was a real delicate little thing. She wanted a tattoo portrait of her dog on her left ankle. That was a challenge. Especially since her dog refused to sit still and kept tryin' to swallow my wrist. She wanted a tattoo of the dog's leash wrapped around her leg to mid-thigh. She came in once a month to add a bush here, a tree there, an occasional flower patch, a park bench, a bus stop. Yep, those calves of hers sure had a story to tell.

My story's all over these walls. Take a look-see. Go ahead. Take a good long look around. I got a snapshot of every last customer that's ever come through the place and gotten inked up. The photos don't come with the place though. I'll be takin' them down directly. I mean, I'll take 'em down before the new owner moves in. That could be you, huh? You could be the next Captain Kich. Go ahead--look around now. You don't have to make up your mind right away. It'll take me a while to get my stuff cleared out. I'd like to throw in my outliner and my shader bars for good measure--if you need 'em. I won't be needin' 'em anymore. I have tatted my last too, so to speak. Can't seem to get a good grip on the old gun these days. My fingers keep tightenin' up. Might just go back to whittlin'. My grandson's a carpenter. Says he's got all kinds of wood for me to work on. Says he'll fix me up with a good workbench on his front porch. I'm not retirin' you see, just slowin' down the pace some. I'll get me another business goin' after a while. Might bring in some of my carvin's to show you one of these days--if you buy the place. Who knows? Maybe we can put 'em up on those shelves over there. Never could figure out what to put on those shelves. Wood carvin's could be just the thing. What do ya say?

THE PITCH

evangelist-type pumps up his sales crew

When a man begins to lose his hair, I feel sorry for him. Don't you? Of course you do. That's why you're here. And that's why every time you knock on a door, it opens, and a man suffering from male pattern baldness appears, I want you to reach down into that wellspring of humanity and try to help him like I know you are all qualified to do. Yes, you must help him with all your Might. When I say Might, you know I mean Might--Magic Might--the skinheads' salvation. Let me hear you say "YEAH!"

Be careful though. These men don't always know who they are but you'll recognize them right off. They're the ones who try to hide it with three strands of hair combed over from behind the ears. You gotta treat these guys with kid gloves or you can forget your daily quota.

This business is tough 'cuz we gotta face facts without the help of our customers. They'll beat around the bush, stutter, stammer and out-and-out deny they got a problem. But you gotta be strong and know that without a conscience, these guys are lost in the woods. Think of yourselves as Jiminy Cricket tap-dancing your way into their empty lives. Pitch 'em good and hard. They'll see the light.

Oh--don't worry about the virile types. You know, the ones who've lost their hair because of too much testosterone? You'll never run into those guys because our listings are fool proof. We get 'em from The See-n-Shop Video Dating Service. It's my brother Dale's company. He finds 'em and I save 'em. Let me hear you say "Yeah!"

RADICAL FLAW

a man blaming his shoes

I don't want my money back. I didn't ask you for my money back. I told you. I want a different pair of shoes--the same brand--a different pair. It's not the brand. I don't want another brand. My girlfriend has this brand and hers work just fine. She can run like the wind. It's obviously the shoes. She never passed me before-- never whipped around the track and put me out of sight before she got these shoes. She got these shoes and now, all of a sudden, her pace has tripled. Since I got these shoes, I can't keep up with her.

I have to have another pair and I have to have this brand. Aries is a great brand but there is something obviously wrong with this particular pair. Actually, it's more devious than obvious because somewhere in this pair of shoes, a radical flaw is hiding. I don't know if it's in the material itself or, perhaps, in the way the design was executed but there is something terribly wrong with this pair. This pair is not optimizing my physiology. I am quicker and stronger and I have mucho stamina compared to this girl--the one who has this same brand of shoe and is humiliating me right out of my sweat pants. I refuse to let this woman race past me in front of my colleagues because of a lousy pair of shoes. This pair of shoes is lousy and her pair is a god-damned cherry.

I would like you to work with me on this because it is in your best interest to produce a satisfied customer. After all, I am a walking adver--I am a running advertisement--or I could be running if you would just trade this faulty pair for a pair that kicks ass. I could sue you for false advertisement. Do you realize that? It's your ads that brought me in here in the first place. I happen to be an Aries and I have always identified with the god of war. I've often thought of myself as a greek god running amok on the planet Mars just like the guy in your ads. You see? You guys got the concept down. You just gotta keep up on your quality control. Somebody turned their cheek when they pooped out this pair and now my girlfriend looks more like your ads than I do.

How many times do I have to tell you? I'm not your guinea pig. This is the last time I'm gonna test run your shoes. Gimme one more pair--one that works--and we're even.